Selling on eBay in 2019

Table of Contents

Introduction

Conclusion

Introduction

Thank you and congratulations on downloading this book.

If you are one of those people who have been tinkering with the idea of making money online for the longest time, you're in for a bit of luck as far as reading this book goes. No, let's rephrase that: you're in for a **pot** of luck, and it's all thanks to the wonderful benefits eBay affords you where it comes to making all the money you ever dreamed of, online.

You might be one of those people with a passion for entrepreneurship, yet you haven't been able to make your foray into an entrepreneurial venture simply because you're too scared of the end results. You might be thinking that you will only end up losing money, and in all probability that has been the very thing that has come in the way of you and your online entrepreneurial success.

The good news as far as selling on eBay is concerned, is the fact that you will not end up losing any money in the process of your online business; you will only end up *making it*. You might have that job security working in a mundane job from 9 to 5 and even though the money is coming in, is that your real passion? Do you like to work for others when you could very well be your own boss and make far more than you are currently earning, via eBay?

In this book you will learn all there is to know about the eBay experience. You will be introduced to all the wonderful tools you need to make that entrepreneurial dream that has been on the backburner for way too long, a tangible reality.

Are you ready, then, to get started and delve into the wonderful **eBay experience**?

Let's get started, then, shall we?

Chapter 1: The Skills & Tools you need to have to sell on eBay

The process of selling on eBay might seem a lot easier than it really is. Here is where you can make a mistake and not focus on the skills and tools that are indispensable where it comes to making your eBay selling experience a notch higher than other eBay sellers out there.

So, what exactly are the things that one needs to take account of, where it comes to making more than just that ephemeral *quick buck* on eBay? Let's find out!

The Skills that one needs to make an impact on the eBay selling process

There are some important skills you need to take note of, where it comes to making a killing selling those products on eBay.

First learn to 'buy'

Buy? You got that right. In the very beginning you need to focus your attention on becoming familiar with the eBay community, by learning how to **buy**. This does not entail that you need to make a purchase, no; all it means is you understand all about the buyer approach. As a buyer, you will find that you can learn all about bidding, PayPal, and how the process of communication between the buyer and the seller, actually works. Thus, it will indirectly broaden your eBay experience.

Sell what you love

Selling becomes a skill when you actually *love* what you are selling. This is because you know your product and appreciate it, and that gives it extra value.

Build your own style

It is important to adapt and customize your profile, and sell in a way that oozes your very own *style*. Through the process of giving a picture of yourself and even writing a short bio, you will become a much better known seller in the eBay community. Furthermore, when you do this you might be able to garner that valuable sense of trust from many buyers out there, who might even buy your product without taking the time to do extra research on your company.

Sell the very same thing, better than your competitors

A lot of times you will be selling the same product as many out there. So, how do you score those extra brownie points with customers? Well, through things like *free shipping* and unparalleled*24 by 7 customer service*, which will only add great value to your business.

Ensure that you choose your words wisely

You have to make sure that you choose your words carefully and use only the very best keywords out there, when you are listing your items on eBay. Now, while it is important that your title is concise, use as many words as you possibly can (*that are descriptive, of course*) so that your item will appear in multiple searches. In fact, the more descriptive you are, the fewer questions you will have to field from those customers. You can also do a search in **eBay** for listings that are similar to yours, and have a lot of activity, in order to come up with something you can add to what you have in mind.

Make sure that your listing is as professional as it can possibly be

The last thing you want is for that listing of yours to look unprofessional and shoddy. So, ensure that apart from having some really snazzy pictures of your product and a description that is clear and well-written, you might wish to use eBay's **listing**

generator and save a template that is sleek and organized, to use for your listings. In fact, you will find that a bulleted list in your description will be most attractive to potential bidders. Also, you will catch a lot more attention with short, informative lines that do not waste your time or even take up a lot of space. Also, ensure that you don't overdo categorization. You will have to pay extra if you are to list your product in multiple categories, so unless you are selling for a whopper of a price, you need to ensure that you pick the *one best* category.

Start those bids low, in order to catch the attention of those bargain hunters.

You will find that while it might be tempting to start a bid at a higher price, it's far more prudent to start your bids low. This will actually help you to get a better sale in the longer run. What a lower bid does, is to catch the attention of more potential buyers and even encourage a competitive bid-off, as the item approaches the last day of bidding. It is important to note here, that this does not apply to products that are really niche. In the case of your item being something that only an avid collector would be looking for, you don't want to make the mistake of setting the initial bid too low, as you are not going to get a lot of bids on an item of this kind. Of course, you could always add a minimum price in case you are worried about getting a rough deal. This means that the product will not be sold unless it reaches the minimum required amount.

Consider free shipping

Free shipping is something that works for some, and a big no-no for others. While the opinions of people might differ on this, free shipping is not actually free, no; you build it into the price of the item. In the case of selling items that will fit into a padded flat rate mailer or box, you can offer free shipping and increase the price of the product by the amount that you will pay for flat rate shipping. However, never make the mistake of offering free shipping on items that are large or heavy.

The Tools you need to make an impact on the eBay selling experience

Apart from skills, here's a look at some valuable *tools* that you can use to sharpen that eBay selling experience

Use eBay autocomplete

When one searches in eBay as a shopper, the search line will also complete your query with the most highly searched for keywords. From your vantage point as a seller, this shows you the items that are most sought after, and their title keywords. In fact, eBay will also suggest the keywords you should include in your title; ensure you make the most of them.

Title Bar

This is a straightforward and easy to use tool, one that helps you get the most searched for title keywords.

Algopix

This is a great tool that will do the price market research for you, automatically. This is better when compared with other market research solutions, because it returns results based on listings that are LIVE, rather than *ended* ones. This, you will find, is essential for correct pricing.

Use the eBay listing tools to add those product identifiers

You will see that product identifiers are critical for the discoverability of a product. What they do, is help eBay build a structured database and better understand what exactly is what, in its humongous database of over abillion products. It is a given that products listed without identifiers will get less and less traffic. So, ensure you make use of these valuable listing tools in order to get your product seen out there!

Use the eBay bulk listing editing tool

While you will find those product identifiers are specific, through the process of using eBay's built-in bulk editing tool you can quickly add identifiers per product, without having to revise the listings individually.

Use the eBay Pulse tool, in order to get to the top of the search results

Of course you want to get to the top of the search results. That would be really cool, wouldn't it? But how on earth does one get there, you might ask? Well, using the eBay Pulse tool that can be downloaded for free online, you will find that you can zone in on the most popular search terms that buyers use. For instance, you will see that *'perfume'* is the second most popular search term in health and beauty after 'Dior', so a listing that is titled 'Dior perfume' will work wonders and will certainly do better than a listing titled, say, 'Dior fragrance'. Use those words well and you might just find yourself at the very top of those search results!

Use the invaluable skills and tools we have discussed above, and you will find you are already a few steps up the ladder where it comes to reaching the peak of your eBay experience.

Chapter 2: What items you should sell on eBay in 2019

If you are looking to make a killing out there by selling products on eBay in the year 2019, then you have to stay relevant. The thing is –

Once trends change, the things that were once popular can now be relegated to *falling out of fashion*.

So, how exactly can one begin the process of researching products – something that will be our best bet where it comes to selling them on eBay? Let's take a look!

Do that research

The very first step, of course, is to actually do that valuable bit of research! This is probably the most time-consuming part of the process, but it is absolutely vital where it comes to deciding what you are going to sell, eventually.

Anyone can sell on eBay, but in order to be successful it takes a good deal of work and thought

There are a few points that one needs to take cognizance of, before zoning in on the actual products that one wishes to sell on eBay in 2019.

Don't be fooled into thinking that 'popular' products mean instant success

On the contrary, the key to successful selling on eBay is to select items *that people really want, that mass sellers don't already target.* Otherwise, you will inadvertently be competing against so many other sellers out there, it will be almost impossible to get your product noticed. Take the instance of **iPhone** covers. Here, you are not only competing against the thousands of people who are trying to sell their own accessories, but also going up against those cheap imports from China. What that means in turn, is that your profit margins would be far below what would be worth the time that is taken to sell/package/post the products.

Create a basic persona of your buyer

What you can do to good effect is to create the persona of the buyer who will be interested in the product you are offering. For instance, if you are selling to young yuppies then you can devise that entire profile around them in order to come up with exactly what they are looking for, like technology, jackets and perhaps even tennis rackets.

Now, while some of these ideas might seem random to you, it's not necessarily a bad thing. The idea is to dish out as many ideas as you possibly can, and then filter them down to a few that might be the exact things you are looking to sell. Then, you can look further into the practicalities of selling your chosen items, in order to see which suits your goals the best.

Find out what is trending on Google

Google is one of the greatest ways in which you can find what people are searching for in that proverbial space called '**out there**'.

So, how can we harness the power of **Google** to our benefit here? Well, all you need to do is use **Google Trends**, which will give you an idea of how popular the item you are looking at selling is, and when it is in highest demand.

Think of the two kinds of products that you wish to sell

You will see that when selling, you can go in for only two kinds of products, really.

1) Commoditized products
2) Niche products

Commoditized products are the ones that everyone needs, and literally the most popular products sold online. They are essentially the ones with the big brand names, like **Nike** and **Fisher-Price**.

Niche products, on the other hand, are goods or services that serve a specific segment of customers. You will see that in many instances they are unique and even *handmade*, making them some of the most sought after products online.

Now, if you offer only commoditized products, especially if they are already big brand names and sold on mega platforms like **Amazon**, you will have a pretty tough time. However, if you can offer unique products alongside those commoditized ones (*here you can try reaching out to customers on Instagram*), you can set yourself up for some really great success.

Sell products that actually solve a problem

Necessity is the mother of invention

How true that is, right? Think of your everyday tasks and what those things are, that come in your way.

These small troubles can actually give way to the best of ideas. All you have to do is pinpoint a problem and *Voila*! You might just have come up with the next **big idea**.

Hop on those trends early

There's a lot of money to be made if you catch those trends early. That is why it is essential that you stay up to date on trending products and services and then capitalize on them before they reach peak popularity.

That being said, here are a few items that are popular to sell on eBay in 2019

Consumer tech from big brands like Apple and Samsung

Believe it or not, but every 14 seconds a tablet is purchased on the site.

On-sale fashion items, like women's dresses

Brands that are popular in particular are **ASOS** and **Topshop**.

Watches

Casio and **Swatch** are amongst the most popular watches sold out there.

Chapter 3: Tips and Tricks to boost your sale on eBay in 2019

By now you have a pretty good idea of what it takes to be a successful seller on eBay, right? Well, be braced for a lot more excitement to come. In this chapter we will learn all about what it takes to ensure we take our sales to the next level altogether, with the invaluable tips and tricks that have been curated especially for you. Are you ready to get started and take a look at them? Why, of course you are! Let's begin then.

The Tips and Tricks that will help boost your sale on eBay

Understand the art of pricing items

Your item price is something that can literally make or break your eBay business. The last thing you need to do is look at retail value, active eBay listings or perhaps even think of how much you paid for an item recently, or a few years ago. What you need to do, then, is to look at completed listings that show historical sales data and not asking prices. This is akin to the process of real estate, where you price your home according to what others have sold their home for, and not what someone is asking.

Start by selling the things you already have

Ever wondered about taking that garbage sale online? Well, with eBay at your side, you most certainly can! You will see that all you have to do is go through your home room-by-room, and look up items on completed listings. You will be surprised to find there are so many things you can start selling, ranging from pots and pans to empty printer cartridges. Ensure here, that you choose only those items that will sell under $50 (*this is because since you are a new seller out there, the last thing you want is to be a target for a scam*). Also, avoid items that easy to ship, and avoid breakables and items with multiple pieces.

Understand your seller limits

This is something that is overlooked by many new sellers out there, but nevertheless something that is most important. In fact, eBay places those selling limits on all sellers, but they are more stringent in the case of new sellers. The idea here is for sellers to establish a *positive selling history*, and the fact that there are limits prevents a certain amount of fraud. So, new sellers will have account limits, category limits and even item limits. Once you have sold a few items, you can then request higher selling limits.

Avoid selling those problematic items

There are some items out there that will always seem to cause after sales problems, and it would be highly prudent you steer clear of selling them when you start out in your eBay business. So, stay away from selling things like iPhones, electronics and even event tickets (*yes, things might just go wrong and events might get cancelled*). What you need to do first, is to establish yourself as a seller of repute, before you go in towards selling these items. Also, you will find that if you sell a designer item on eBay and it is a fake (*like perhaps a handbag*), you can be suspended in the very first instance.

Ensure you get the right supplies

You don't really need to have a lot of expensive equipment to sell on eBay. All you really need is the following:

1) 2 pieces of plain white poster board that will help you make a solid background for those photos.
2) A scale for weighing items when listing and shipping
3) Shipping supplies – here you will find that you can get free priority supplies from **USPS**, or even order polymailers on eBay for first class shipping.

Take a lot of photographs

People out there will be able to tell the difference between stock images and the genuine thing, so ensure you take a good photograph of the product *as-is*. This will ensure that the customer gains that vital sense of confidence where it comes to buying your product.

Get your timing right

You will find that according to eBay,

The busiest time for sales is Sunday evening

So, make sure you cash in on that opportunity by scheduling your auctions to end around then. Also, ensure you avoid those times when a lot of people will be busy, such as weekday mornings or even around big sports games.

Make sure that your postage process is as prompt as possible

The last thing you want to is to annoy that buyer that has paid for next – day delivery, and then have them wait for three days to get your product. You have to deliver as promised, so ensure you ship as soon as possible and avoid those bad reviews.

Give that refund where it is due

You don't wish for an irate customer to give you a negative review, so if your item arrives damaged because it was insufficiently packed, or if you didn't accurately describe it, remember that the customer is always right and ensure that you give that refund!

Be sure to promote yourself well

If you are selling a lot of products in the same category, you could include a note or a flyer with shipped items that will alert the customer to other products they might be interested in.

Choose the right listing type

This can be extremely important where it comes to making the sale in the most effective manner. You have to discern whether you are going to be selling that item as an '*auction*' item or at a fixed price. There are advantages and disadvantages of both these types of listings. Also, auctions are no longer what they used to be on eBay, so make sure that you start them at an acceptable price. The fixed price listings might take longer to sell, but you will find that if you wait for the right buyer, you can get the high price you have commanded.

Chapter 4: What to do when an item sells on eBay

Whether your business is custom-coated widgets, or perhaps even personalized software of some kind, you will find that there is nothing quite like that *'Item Sold!'* email that you get moments after the product has been purchased.

In most instances, you will find that collecting money on items sold on eBay is an automatic process, in which you are often paid before you even know it. However, on occasion you have to rely on eBay's features, in order to complete the transaction.

Here are a few quick tips that will help ensure that you do exactly the right thing after your item sells on eBay.

Check your email for that Notice of Auction Closure or Buy it Now Completion

These are the things that are automatically generated by eBay, so that both the buyer and seller are informed of the purchase. Furthermore, eBay also sends the auction winner an invoice. What you need to do is to check your email shortly after the sale, as there are some buyers that pay immediately, especially if they were bidding repeatedly at the end.

Review your my eBay page

Then, what you need to do is to scroll to an item that is awaiting payment, click on 'Action', and then click 'Send Invoice'. It should be noted here that eBay would have already totaled all of the charges, taxes, shipping fees and even the additional items that you would have set up while creating that auction. Here you can also include a note to the seller to the tune of *'Please pay within three business days'*.

Contact eBay, in the case of not being paid for an item, through its Resolution Center

This, in fact, is your final way in which you can procure that payment, because what eBay does is to generate a warning message to the buyer. It also ensures that you do not have to pay the final item fees - the fees that eBay charges you for the money you collect from selling a product.

The next step, of course, is shipping the product

It is absolutely imperative to get a good idea of when you should actually be shipping your product to the customer who has purchased it. Here are a few things that you need to bear in mind, during this process.

Check the 'Transaction Details' area of the details page. If the status is '**Ok to ship**', then it is safe to assume that your buyer's payment has cleared, the funds have been transferred to your PayPal account and the Seller Protection (*in case the item is eligible for it*) is active for the sale. You should immediately ship out your item in this instance.

If you see '**Don't Ship Yet**', then that means that eBay and/or PayPal have seen something about the buyer or transaction that they don't like. It might even mean that the payment has not yet cleared.

It is important to note here, that some forms of electronic payment can take several days to clear, and this is not necessarily cause for alarm. Of course, it can be a source of very real frustration for the sellers out there who want quick access to funds. So, when you see this status, your role as a seller is to wait until the status changes for the better.

Stop – Don't Ship. In this case, you know that eBay or PayPal wants this sale undone. This is because either the payment did not clear (*in which case you will not be receiving any funds in your account, of course*) or it was perhaps because the buyer has been deemed to be ineligible to make this purchase on eBay. In the case of the latter, it's often on account of a suspension of some kind that took place during the course of your transaction with them.

After the product has been successfully shipped, you might wish to leave some valuable feedback for the people who have purchased your product. It is important to note here that any feedback that you leave is **public** and **permanent**, so make sure that your comments are fair and factual. In the case of a dispute, you need to try and resolve your differences before leaving that vital feedback.

Of course, eBay does not charge for most listings out there, but they will charge a fee (*or a commission*), once your item has been sold to your buyer. If you look to the bottom of the page, there will be a note telling you the details.

So, it is really not all that difficult where it comes to the process that ensues after you make a sale on eBay. As has been effectively pointed out in this chapter, you need to tread those waters carefully, in order to ensure that you do not actually end up losing money, instead of making it.

Chapter 5: Optimizing Shipping

So, you have made that all important sale of yours online, to your very first customer. While that might surely be a great thing, there is still some work left to be done. You have to ship that sold item to your buyer quickly, without the risk of it getting damaged. While in the previous chapter we have seen all about the importance of knowing when to ship the product to the buyer, in this chapter we will take a look at the *how* of the shipping process, and look at ways in which we can optimize the experience!

Optimizing shipping for your sales on eBay

Here's a look at some really great ways in which you can make that shipping experience pack that proverbial punch.

Work out those shipping costs

Shipping costs depend on a variety of factors, like

1) *Weight and dimensions of the package.*
2) *The method of shipment – airmail, surface mail or speed post.*
3) *The location that you are shipping from.*
4) *The location that you are shipping to.*
5) *Whether you include insurance or if the carrier includes it automatically.*

In the case of shipping internationally, it is usually the buyer that pays for shipping and any other additional costs that are incurred in the process, like insurance, duties and taxes. There are even some instances where an 'extended area surcharge' might apply to your buyers, depending on where they are located internationally.

It's a really great idea to include a *handling charge* in the shipping cost, in order to cover your time and expenses. Make sure that you specify, though, that the cost includes a handling charge and is not just postage. In the case that you don't, there are some buyers that might feel ripped off when they see that the postage only cost $4 and you charged $6. It is most certainly fair to cover these costs, especially since your time is involved in packaging and posting the item. In order to get people out there to accept this small charge even more readily, all you have to do is itemize the handling cost, instead of merely including it with shipping.

Furthermore, ensure that you don't overdo the shipping costs. It is against eBay's rules, to go out there and make profit on shipping rather than on the item itself. In fact, this policy has been exploited so many times in the past, that eBay recently introduced the policy of removing those auctions with outsized shipping charges.

Customs

There are a lot of small items for which many sellers get around the process of having to pay those custom charges, by sending it as a gift. So, it is most prudent to research the areas that you are going to be sending your items to. There are certain places that have some really unusual restrictions on items, and you most probably wouldn't have known about these if you hadn't checked. For instance. Italy doesn't allow shoes and Australia does not allow used bedding!

Always include a packing slip in your package

You never know if there is something wrong that is going to happen to that package of yours, and as long as there is a packing slip, you can rest assured that the shipper can still deliver the package or even send it back to you. In that way, you won't have a problem if the shipping label is torn off or even unreadable.

Ensure that you use delivery confirmation on all your packages

There are some shady buyers out there online, who will claim they haven't received your parcel, even if they did. Therefore, ensure you use delivery confirmation on all packages. When you do, you are assured those shady buyers will think twice before claiming that they haven't received your parcel.

Get shipping insurance

This is really important, and something that can be easily overlooked. You have to ensure that you get that shipping insurance for expensive items, even if the buyer did not pay for it. The thing is, things can get broken and even lost during shipping, and you need to be protected financially, if the buyer wants their money back in such instances.

Get a thermal label printer

This is not really required, but something you could do well with. In the case of you doing a lot of shipping, it will make the printing of labels much easier. What's more, the labels are self-adhesive and can be ordered free from**UPS**. All you have to do is peel the labels off and stick them on the box to be shipped.

Use the buyer's integrated shipping tool

In case the buyer uses PayPal, you can very well use their *integrated shipping tool.* You will find that when you go to print the label, the buyer's shipping address is automatically added to the label along with the weight and insurance, in case applicable. What this does, really, is to save you the trouble of entering the information yourself. Once that label has been printed, you will find that you can print a packing slip with all the key information that has been filled in earlier. You will see that the postage amount can be hidden on the label, and you can print both USPS and UPS labels using PayPal.

It's really not that big a deal when it comes to shipping your product after all, is it?

Chapter 6: Impressing your Customers

In the end, it's about providing a **bespoke experience** for your client; one that will make him or her always gravitate towards your site where it comes to making those vital online purchases, as well as attracting a flood of new customers. Therefore, you have to ensure you pull all stops in the process of creating an experience for the customer that will actually have a strong impact on him or her.

In the end, you want them to buy your product from you, rather than you having to sell it to them.

So, how do we impress those customers with a view to ensuring they prefer the buying experience with *us* as compared to the large numbers of sellers out there? Let's take a peek, shall we?

Some really stellar tips on how to woo your Customers on eBay in 2019

Here's a look at how you can ensure you hit that proverbial nail on its head where it comes to impressing your customers with a sense of élan.

Get the three essentials absolutely right in order to create a really great first impression

So, what's the big deal about that first impression anyways? Well, it might just be the clinching factor where it comes to procuring a new customer. Let's look at the 3 absolutely essential ingredients that combine to create a stellar impression on your customers.

Create professional product images

We have already seen that we need *real* pictures instead of mere *stock images*, but if you want to take it one notch higher, ensure the images are well shot and capturedwith a professional camera.

Provide accurate descriptions of your product

People know when you are accurately describing your product and when you are making it sound better than it really is. So, ensure you stick to the *actual details* of the product. You might think telling a lie is all right, but it most certainly is not, especially when people are investing their money in your product.

Offer a return policy that is fair

You will find that many new sellers do not like the idea of having a return policy, but according to the **eBay Guarantee**, all sellers have one whether they like it or not. In fact, eBay rewards those sellers who have a 30-day or longer return policy, by giving them a boost in their product search results. Therefore, it would behoove you to have a fair return policy that will only serve to build that valuable sense of trust between your customer and you.

Conclusion

In this book we have learned all that there is to know about selling on eBay in 2019. We have seen everything from the tricks of the trade, to the nitty-gritties of the selling process that will ensure that we become maestros at the art of selling on eBay.

The thing is, there is a vast amount of competition these days; indeed, a lot more than there used to be in the days when eBay had just started out. That makes it all the more important, then, to leave absolutely no stone unturned, where it comes to making that eBay buying experience several notches higher than the rest of the people out there who are trying as hard as you are, to push their products.

In the end, selling on eBay is a business venture just like any other and when you treat it with a sense of professionalism and use all the tricks and tools that you have gleaned over the course of reading this book, you will soon find yourself in pristine company, hobnobbing in the virtual space out there with other stalwarts of the **eBay business club**.

Are you ready, then, to get started and make that eBay venture of yours every bit of the success you wish it to be?

Well, what are you waiting for? Begin your foray into the wonderful world of selling on eBay, now!

Copyright

Made in the USA
Middletown, DE
18 February 2019